SPACE DOCTRINE PUBLICATION 1-0

PERSONNEL DOCTRINE FOR SPACE FORCES

UNITED STATES SPACE FORCE

NIMBLE BOOKS LLC: THE AI LAB FOR BOOK-LOVERS

Humans and AI making books richer, more diverse, and more surprising.

PUBLISHING INFORMATION

(c) 2023 Nimble Books LLC
ISBN: 978-1-60888-211-3

AI-GENERATED KEYWORD PHRASES

⇒ Space Force;
⇒ Space Force Bases;
⇒ Space Doctrine;
⇒ USSF;
⇒ Air Force Manpower;
⇒ Air Force Research;
⇒ USSF Personnel Organizations;
⇒ USSF Space Base;
⇒ Force Development;
⇒ Personnel]

ABSTRACTS

TL;DR (ONE WORD)

Guardians.

SYNOPSIS

This document is the Space Doctrine Publication 1-0 for the United States Space Force (USSF). It provides guidance for the development and employment of USSF personnel, covering topics such as organization, force development, resilience, and global perspective. It outlines the roles and responsibilities of various USSF commands and personnel organizations and emphasizes the importance of personnel readiness and resilience in supporting the USSF's mission. The document also discusses the USSF's approach to force development, including recruitment, training, education, and experience-based development, and the use of developmental teams. It also mentions the consideration of personal circumstances and aspirations in promotion and assignment decisions.

Visual

Prompt: Please create an illustration that conveys the message of this document without words. ChatGPT.

Space Force has some of the most daunting personnel development challenges of any military organization. Present and future Guardians must learn to operate effectively in dizzyingly complex and dynamic environment. In the spirit of the AI Lab for Book-Lovers, this illustration is provided to illustrate one potential new tool for personnel education: *visual abstracting.*

Here, from the prompt provided in the caption, LLM has drawn on the content of the document and created an image that has many subtle cues to convey its message.

1. The image is set in the future in a "next-gen" or "next-next-gen" military space station: Space Force is developing personnel for the long term.

2. There are a large number of team members arranged in an egalitarian layout: Space Force is not about solo heroes.

3. People are well equipped with computing technology. Apparently, tablets and laptops are still a thing.

4. Many are wearing helmets, suggesting that future Guardians must be ready to operate in combat-ready environments near the "front". No FOBBITs here!

5. The command table is circular and offers a top-down view of Earth, perhaps a feed from a polar satellite, while the orbital windows offer a different view of a continental shelf passing below. Guardians will need to synthesize many competing inputs.

6. A grey-haired general is visible at ten o'clock. This is still the military.

PAGE-BY-PAGE SUMMARIES

1   The Space Doctrine Publication 1-0, Personnel, is a publication by the United States Space Force that provides guidance and information on personnel matters in the space domain.

2   Space Doctrine Publication 1-0, Personnel, provides guidance on the development and sustainment of personnel in the United States Space Force (USSF). It emphasizes the importance of personnel readiness and resilience in fulfilling USSF's responsibilities. The publication addresses the role of various forces, including Guardians and other personnel, in supporting USSF missions.

3   This page is a table of contents for a document titled "Space Doctrine Publication 1-0, Personnel." It includes chapters on the introduction, USSF organization, force development, Guardian resilience, global perspective, and USAF support to the USSF.

4   This page introduces the Space Doctrine Publication 1-0, Personnel, which focuses on the development and support of personnel in the United States Space Force (USSF). It emphasizes the importance of Guardians (personnel) and their diverse skills and experiences. The publication also addresses the essential support provided by personnel from the Department of the Air Force and Air National Guard. It highlights the force development process, individual resilience programs, and the need for a global perspective.

5   Space Doctrine Publication 1-0, Personnel, published on 7 September 2022, provides guidance and information on personnel matters in the field of space operations.

6   The page discusses the organizational structure of the United States Space Force (USSF), including the three field commands and their roles in delivering space capabilities. The top three leaders of the USSF are also mentioned.

7   This page provides an overview of the personnel organizations within the United States Space Force (USSF), including STARCOM, SSC, OCSO, CHCO, and FIELDCOM. It explains their responsibilities in terms of education, training, doctrine, recruitment, retention, and force management.

8   The page discusses the personnel support structure within the Space Force, including the role of Delta units, Space Base Deltas, and the Space Force Element. It also introduces the concept of a Component Field Command as the organizational structure for integrating space operations into joint forces.

9   Force development in the Space Doctrine Publication 1-0 focuses on creating opportunities for personnel to determine their career paths and

20   This page discusses the importance of developing a global perspective for Guardians in order to provide innovative solutions and effects in space. It highlights the need for joint integration and partnerships with allies and partners to enhance deterrence, protect mutual interests, and build capability in the space domain.

21   This page discusses various programs and roles within the United States Space Force (USSF) that involve international partnerships, cultural exchange, and collaboration with other organizations. These include mobile training teams, military personnel exchange programs, liaison officers, security cooperation officers, study abroad programs, and the Regional Space Advisor (RSA) Program. Additionally, the page mentions the importance of interagency, industry, and academic engagements for strengthening USSF capabilities.

22   The Space Doctrine Publication 1-0 discusses the University Partnership Program (UPP) and University Consortium (UC) initiatives of the United States Space Force (USSF). These programs aim to establish partnerships with universities, promote research and development in space-related fields, and develop a diverse and highly competent workforce. The USSF collaborates with academic institutions, government labs, and private industry to enhance security and advance capabilities in the space domain.

23   This page discusses the personnel serving in the United States Space Force (USSF), including active-duty Airmen, DAF civilians, Air Force Reservists, and Air National Guardsmen. It highlights their roles and responsibilities in executing the space mission and supporting USSF organizations.

24   The page discusses how the US Air Force (USAF) provides personnel support to the US Space Force (USSF), including legal, religious affairs, finance, and other functions. It also mentions the involvement of the Air Force Reserve Command (AFRC) and National Guard Bureau (NGB) in supporting USSF operations. The USSF is working on developing processes and policies to ensure seamless integration of space professionals from the AFR and ANG into its forces.

25   This page provides a list of acronyms and abbreviations related to personnel in the Space Doctrine Publication 1-0.

26   The page provides a list of abbreviations and acronyms related to space doctrine, personnel, and organizations within the United States Air Force and Space Force.

Notable Passages

1   "Space Doctrine Publication (SDP) 1-0, Personnel United States Space Force (USSF)"

2   "Personnel readiness and resilience enables the USSF to provide trained and ready forces, including Guardians, Active-duty Airmen, Department of the Air Force (DAF) civilians, Air Force Reservists, and Air National Guardsman. These forces contribute to prompt and sustained space operations that fulfill the cornerstone responsibilities of the USSF: preserve freedom of action, enable joint lethality and effectiveness, and provide independent options. SDP 1-0, while focused on Guardians, addresses the role of all these forces in enabling the USSF mission by ensuring a common presentation of forces to combatant commanders, and preservation of capability among forces performing space missions."

4   "Our greatest assets are the individuals—Guardians—who develop, protect, sustain, employ, and advance spacepower for the nation. Sound doctrine and superior capabilities are of little use without personnel who have the expertise and empowerment required to implement them."

5   "Space is a complex and dynamic domain that is critical to our national security and the global economy. As space becomes increasingly congested, contested, and competitive, it is essential that we have a comprehensive understanding of the space environment and the ability to effectively operate within it. This requires a clear and coherent space doctrine that guides our actions and informs our decision-making processes.

Our space doctrine must address a wide range of challenges and opportunities, including space situational awareness, space control, space force enhancement, space support, and space force application. It must also consider the unique characteristics of space, such as the absence of gravity, the vacuum of space, and the vast distances involved.
By developing and implementing a robust space doctrine, we can ensure that our space capabilities are effectively integrated into our overall military strategy and that we are able to protect and defend our interests in space. This will require a coordinated effort across all branches of the military, as well as close collaboration with our international partners.

6   "The USSF is responsible for organizing, training, and equipping its personnel, while ensuring they are ready and qualified to integrate with the joint force. In the USSF's first planning guidance publication, the Chief of Space Operations (CSO) directed the use of mission command and established his intent for the nation's newest military branch to operate as an empowered, lean, and agile service. This direction translates to a streamlined organizational structure supporting the employment of Guardians at locations around the globe."

7   "The CHCO (SF/S1) assists the SecAF and the CSO by developing policies, programs, and processes for the recruitment, employment, organization, professional development, and retention of personnel to meet USSF manpower requirements. The USSF Talent Management Office (TMO) engages with Guardians to develop and effectively employ their talents from recruitment to retirement or separation. Offices under the CHCO develop USSF Total Force policy and guidance, and identify

manpower and personnel requirements. They create and review personnel policies, guidance, programs, and legislative initiatives. Offices under the CHCO work with multiple Air Force offices and the Air Force Personnel Center (AFPC) to oversee manpower, policy, and management for Guardians."

8   "Space Force components will play an important role integrating space capabilities into joint operations in every domain and every area of responsibility."

9   "For a Guardian there is no single pathway or definition of career success. Combining training, education, and experiential learning, the USSF works to produce the balance of expertise and competence needed to satisfy operational requirements and meet the CSO's priority to develop warfighters in world-class teams. The USSF invests in individuals and, as feasible, matches their interests, strengths, and potential with the Service's current and future needs."

10   "The USSF uses a comprehensive and individualized approach to personnel development supported by centralized and concurrent boards for promotions, assignments, education, command selection, performance-based retention, development program matches, competency framework adjustments, diversity, and recruiting needs in accordance with all applicable laws and policies."

11   "An individual's competencies and experiences drive progress through the training process and achievement of higher tiers of expertise."

12   "The Ready Spacecrew Program focuses on enhancing knowledge and warfighting capability of space forces. Advanced training courses address operational TTPs that include cyberspace and intelligence to prepare space forces to integrate effects across multiple domains and achieve weapon system mastery."

13   "Guardian Supra Coders, having completed an intensive software engineering curriculum, become members of agile software development product teams in the field so they can develop, deploy, and update software that works for its users at the speed of mission need."

14   "Space Doctrine Publication 1-0, Personnel

Officer Academy, Senior Noncommissioned Officer Academy, Squadron Officer School, Air Command, and Staff College – Schriever Space Scholars, School of Advanced Air and Space Studies, Air War College – West Space Seminar, and the Joint Professional Military Education courses support Guardians as they progress through the ranks."

15   "Experience contributes to an individual's development in ways that neither training nor education can. Diverse experiences enable Guardians to be more effective team members."

16   "Engagements with allies and partners through wargames and exercises."

17   "Resilience — an individual's capacity to recover from hardship or difficulties — is a critical element of readiness. People can develop the ability to withstand, adapt to, and recover from stress and adversity by using effective coping strategies. Thus, strengthening resilience has a direct impact on the lethality and effectiveness of a warfighting unit."

18   "Each member of our team shares in the enduring responsibility to eliminate sexual assault and harassment from our ranks. I urge every

Airman, Guardian, and Department civilian to treat each other with dignity and respect, hold others accountable to our high standards of conduct, and to take care of your teammates." SecAF Frank Kendall, 27 April 2022"

19   "ESport is a program designed to bolster resilience, forge camaraderie, and hone warrior-lethality in preparation for the future fight."

20   "Guardians must develop and maintain a global perspective in order to provide innovative solutions and spacepower effects for the US and our allies. Guardians must be sufficiently agile to leverage joint, interagency, allied, civil, and/or commercial resources. Our global persistence and enduring vigilance posture the joint force to assure allies, deter aggression, coerce competitors, and defeat adversaries. USSF training, education, and readiness inculcate Guardians with an understanding of joint planning, doctrine, and partnerships/engagements (multinational, interagency, academia, and industry) in order to advance national priorities as part of the joint force."

21   "Regional Space Advisor (RSA) Program. The RSA Program identifies and prepares a select group of Guardians for direct interaction with allies and partners. RSAs form a cadre of Guardian leaders deliberately developed to enhance USSF capabilities by evolving and expanding partnerships to strengthen relationships, secure common interests, and promote shared values in space. As a career-broadening program, USSF expects RSAs to demonstrate proficiency in a core space discipline and receive additional training to increase their personal leadership competencies. With advanced knowledge of space policies and political-military affairs, regional and cultural expertise, and demonstrated language proficiency (as needed), the USSF assigns RSA to key strategic billets. In those roles, RSAs implement campaign support plans and inject, track, and assess the USSF's space domain interests within both regional theater security cooperation plans, and allied and partner nation activities."

22   "The aim is to collaborate, as permitted by law and policy, on the long and short-term science and technology (S&T) problem sets; and to promote partnerships with academic institutions, government labs, and private industry. This collaborative and inclusive approach allows the USSF to promote and strengthen strategic relationships to deliver new capabilities at operationally relevant speeds that enhance security and preserve prosperity of the space domain."

23   "The USSF, as part of the DAF, employs Guardians, active-duty Airmen, DAF civilians, Air Force Reservists and Air National Guardsmen to execute the space mission."

24   "USAF organizations provide many of the personnel functions for Guardians and USAF, AFR, and ANG personnel assigned to USSF units or Space Force Bases. In addition to the personnel support functions detailed below, USAF also provides legal, religious affairs, finance, contracting, meteorological, and mortuary affairs support to Guardians."

25   "Chief Master Sergeant of the Space Force"

26   "Morale, Welfare, and Recreation"

Space Doctrine Publication 1-0

PERSONNEL

DOCTRINE FOR SPACE FORCES

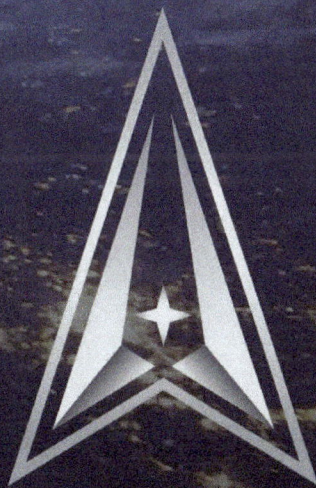

UNITED STATES
SPACE FORCE

Space Doctrine Publication (SDP) 1-0, *Personnel*
United States Space Force (USSF)
7 September 2022

Foreword

United States Space Force (USSF) doctrine guides the development and employment of Guardians in support of the Service's cornerstone responsibilities. A body of carefully developed and sanctioned ideas, doctrine establishes a common framework for understanding and applying USSF capabilities. This doctrine provides official advice and describes the best way to develop and sustain Guardians throughout their careers. By its nature, doctrine is not directive, and instead provides the USSF an informed starting point for decision-making and strategy development.

Space Doctrine Publication (SDP) 1-0, *Personnel*, aligns with current USSF doctrine and Chief of Space Operations' Planning Guidance. SDP 1-0 articulates the current USSF structure, the contributions of external agencies to the USSF, and best practices for force development and sustainment unique to the Guardian culture.

Personnel readiness and resilience enables the USSF to provide trained and ready forces, including Guardians, Active-duty Airmen, Department of the Air Force (DAF) civilians, Air Force Reservists, and Air National Guardsman. These forces contribute to prompt and sustained space operations that fulfill the cornerstone responsibilities of the USSF: preserve freedom of action, enable joint lethality and effectiveness, and provide independent options. SDP 1-0, while focused on Guardians, addresses the role of all these forces in enabling the USSF mission by ensuring a common presentation of forces to combatant commanders, and preservation of capability among forces performing space missions.

Many years of developing space personnel allows our doctrine to speak from a position of authority. I encourage you to study and learn from the time-tested knowledge compiled in this publication. Semper Supra!

BRATTON.SH
AWN.N.11872
76787

Digitally signed by
BRATTON.SHAWN.N.11
87276787
Date: 2022.09.07
13:15:28 -06'00'

SHAWN N. BRATTON
Major General, USAF
Commander, Space Training and Readiness Command

Table of Contents

Table of Figures

Chapter 1: Introduction

Our greatest assets are the individuals—Guardians—who develop, protect, sustain, employ, and advance spacepower for the nation. Sound doctrine and superior capabilities are of little use without personnel who have the expertise and empowerment required to implement them. The responsibility of the United States Space Force (USSF), like its sister services, is to organize, train, and equip forces to support the joint force commander conducting operations across the competition continuum (as defined in Joint Doctrine Note 1-19, *Competition Continuum*, 3 June 2019).

The USSF prioritizes the development and sustainment of Guardians, which include active-duty officers and enlisted personnel, and civilians, allowing the service to capitalize on the diversity of its personnel, along with their skills, talents, expertise, and perspective. Additionally, personnel transitioning from sister services bring with them rich experiences that are invaluable to shaping the culture, heritage, and expertise of the USSF and its ability to present capabilities and forces to the joint force.

While Guardians are the primary focus of this publication, the USSF recognizes that personnel from elsewhere in the Department of the Air Force (DAF) (active duty, reservists and civilians) and Air National Guard are essential to all areas of the USSF mission. They provide essential support to USSF Space Base Deltas and Space Force Bases. Chapter 6 addresses these essential service partners.

SDP 1-0, *Personnel*, addresses the USSF organizations that develop and support Guardians (including assigned civilians) throughout their careers (Chapter 2). The force development process addressed in Chapter 3, and programs supporting individual resilience addressed in Chapter 4, combine to ensure personnel are equipped with the leadership, weapons systems, skill sets, personal resilience, and foresight necessary to protect and defend interests of the United States (US) and its allies in any strategic or operational environment. Chapter 5 also addresses the need for every Guardian to develop and maintain a global perspective as part of their professional development.

This doctrine publication is official advice, and commanders should follow it except when, in their judgment, circumstances dictate otherwise. Doctrine reflects fundamental principles and best practices based on extant capabilities. It incorporates changes derived from lessons learned during operations, training, wargames, exercises, and, when appropriate, validated concepts.

The USSF is rapidly developing in every area and personnel practices are no exception. Where the USSF is developing new policies, processes, or structures, such as the *Guardian Ideal*, call-out boxes (light blue boxes with rounded corners) highlight those for the reader. As the USSF implements these changes, Space Training and Readiness Command (STARCOM) Delta 10 will update this publication.

Guardian Ideal

Published on 17 September 2021, the *Guardian Ideal* is the USSF's Human Capital Strategy, and explains how the USSF intends to attract and develop talent. The USSF will move to a regulated market approach to talent management that integrates and strengthens equity, development, and human dignity. It will empower individuals to pursue pathways that are informed by both their preferences and an understanding of Space Force requirements–unleashing the potential of *every* Guardian..

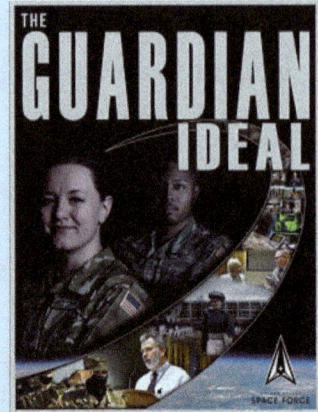

Chapter 2: USSF Organization

The USSF is responsible for organizing, training, and equipping its personnel, while ensuring they are ready and qualified to integrate with the joint force. In the USSF's first planning guidance publication, the Chief of Space Operations (CSO) directed the use of mission command and established his intent for the nation's newest military branch to operate as an empowered, lean, and agile service. This direction translates to a streamlined organizational structure supporting the employment of Guardians at locations around the globe.

USSF Structure

Three Field Commands (FIELDCOMs), Space Operations Command (SpOC), Space Systems Command (SSC) and STARCOM, support the Office of the Chief of Space Operations (OCSO). Forces assigned to OCSO, Space Base Deltas, FIELDCOMs, and their subordinate units (Deltas and Directorates) deliver space capabilities to the warfighter. The top three Guardians—the CSO, Vice Chief of Space Operations (VCSO) and Chief Master Sergeant of the Space Force (CMSSF)—lead the USSF.

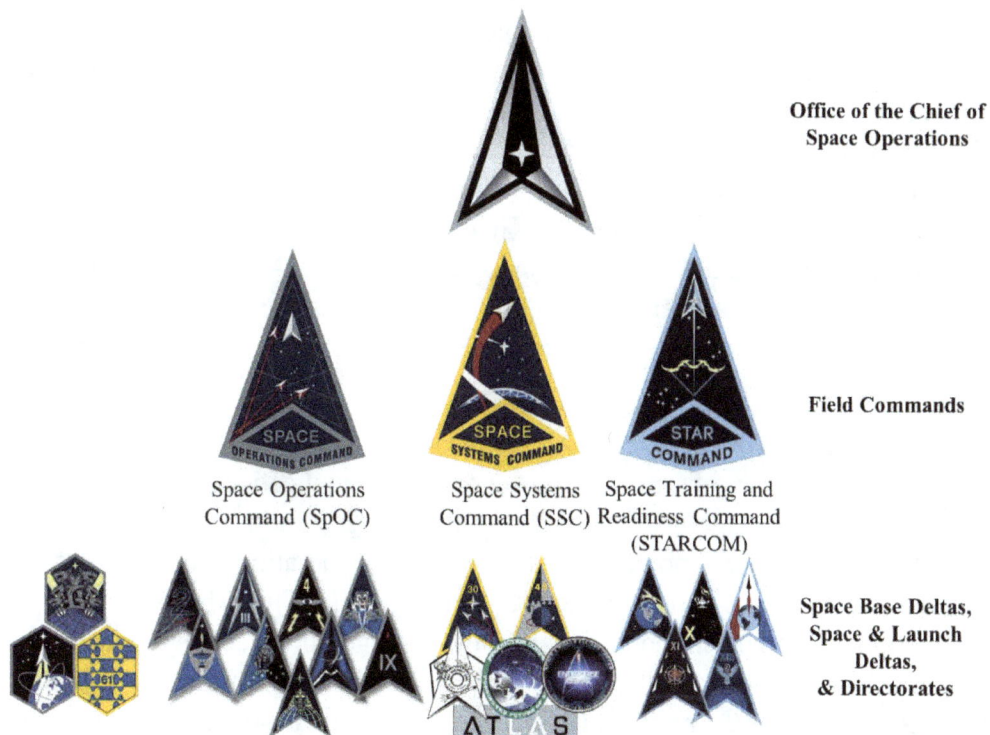

Figure 1. USSF structure

a. **SpOC.** SpOC generates, presents, and sustains combat-ready Guardians for space operations, intelligence, cyberspace, and combat support missions.

b. **STARCOM.** STARCOM is responsible for preparing every Guardian to prevail in competition and conflict by developing and conducting education, training, doctrine, wargaming, lessons learned, test, and evaluation.

c. **SSC.** SSC is responsible for delivering new space capabilities at operationally relevant speeds, to include developing, acquiring, equipping, fielding, and sustaining those capabilities. SSC builds, launches, and sustains space capabilities for military and civilian users worldwide.

USSF Personnel Organizations

a. **OCSO.** OCSO staff establishes policy, assigns responsibilities, and prescribes procedures for USSF personnel readiness. The VCSO implements plans, programs, and policies for managing the USSF and all Guardians. The CMSSF advises and assists the CSO and Secretary of the Air Force (SecAF) on matters concerning enlisted Guardians.

b. **Chief Human Capital Officer (CHCO).** The CHCO (SF/S1) assists the SecAF and the CSO by developing policies, programs, and processes for the recruitment, employment, organization, professional development, and retention of personnel to meet USSF manpower requirements. The USSF Talent Management Office (TMO) engages with Guardians to develop and effectively employ their talents from recruitment to retirement or separation. Offices under the CHCO develop USSF Total Force policy and guidance, and identify manpower and personnel requirements. They create and review personnel policies, guidance, programs, and legislative initiatives. Offices under the CHCO work with multiple Air Force offices and the Air Force Personnel Center (AFPC) to oversee manpower, policy, and management for Guardians. Specific Air Force offices include the Assistant Secretary of the Air Force Manpower & Reserve Affairs (SAF/MR), Air Force Manpower, Personnel and Services (AF/A1), and the Assistant Secretary of the Air Force for Acquisition, Technology, and Logistics (SAF/AQ) (for those in the Acquisition Demonstration program).

c. **FIELDCOM and Separate Units' Manpower and Personnel Offices.** The FIELDCOM and separate units' manpower and personnel offices execute military and civilian personnel management in support of those organizations' missions and priorities. These offices develop manpower inputs by providing operational assessments on required systems and capabilities that facilitate the planning cycle. The FIELDCOM and separate units' manpower and personnel offices are also engaged in force development for all Guardians. These offices are also responsible for readiness program management including Air Reserve Component (ARC) activations and mobilizations, continuity of operations plans, reporting instructions and accountability, deployment discrepancies, and force presentation management.

d. **Deltas and Space Base Deltas Personnel Support**. Guardians assigned to a Delta rely on their supporting FIELDCOM, Space Base Deltas, installation Force Support Squadron, and the USSF TMO for personnel and manpower transactions.

e. **Space Force Element (SFELM).** SFELMs consist of Guardians on duty with organizations outside the DAF (e.g., the National Reconnaissance Office, and combatant commands). Guardians assigned to an SFELM may rely on a FIELDCOM or the SF/S1 for manpower and personnel functions.

Component Field Command

Like any other military service, the Space Force will prepare to present forces to every combatant command. Service components are the primary building blocks of every joint force. In accordance with joint doctrine, Space Force components will be the organizational structures through which Guardians will integrate into the joint force. A component field command (C-FLDCOM) will integrate space operations at the component level, conducting military operations under the delegated authorities of a combatant commander. Space Force components will play an important role integrating space capabilities into joint operations in every domain and every area of responsibly.

Chapter 3: Force Development

Force development is the deliberate effort to establish an opportunity-rich environment for personnel to determine their career path. It helps build Guardians ready to execute the Service's cornerstone responsibilities in all domains and to outpace our adversaries. It depends on dynamic processes that integrate and synchronize senior leader perspectives and organizational needs to forecast qualitative and quantitative requirements for the service.

The desired outcome of force development is to increase readiness, and ensure Guardians are equipped and trained for their missions. Force development for all Guardians begins with recruiting followed by robust training, education, and experience to develop a skilled, resilient, and solution-oriented workforce.

For a Guardian there is no single pathway or definition of career success. Combining training, education, and experiential learning, the USSF works to produce the balance of expertise and competence needed to satisfy operational requirements and meet the CSO's priority to develop warfighters in world-class teams. The USSF invests in individuals and, as feasible, matches their interests, strengths, and potential with the Service's current and future needs.

> **Guardian Values**
>
> Essential to force development is instilling each Guardian with USSF values. *The Guardian Values Handbook* will formalize and support institutionalization of the USSF values. Guardian values will serve as the foundation of our culture and identity as Guardians.
>
> *Character... above all*
> *Connection... toward unity*
> *Commitment... to mastery*
> *Courage... to be bold*

Guardian Development

Talent management and employment of Guardians includes training, education, and experience-based development, enabling continuing professional development over the entirety of an individual's career. Building on the foundational knowledge provided through training and education, and solidified with practice and experience, every individual receives tailored developmental opportunities. This approach allows each Guardian flexibility in accessing available resources, maximizing their potential as they establish their career path. This process also allows the USSF to capitalize fully on a Guardian's knowledge and previous experience. The USSF TMO divisions each focus on an aspect of talent management and operations.

    a. **Guardian Generation**. Guardian Generation focuses on recruiting talent, hiring, onboarding, inter-service transfers, and ensuring engagement with Guardians.

b. **Guardian Development**. Guardian Development manages the competency framework, oversees developmental programs such as mentoring and coaching, and manages the talent management related boards.

c. **Guardian Employment.** Guardian Employment, along with AFPC, orchestrates Guardian assignments and use of Department of Defense (DOD), DAF, and United States Air Force (USAF), programs.

d. **Studies and Analysis.** Studies and Analysis employs data and people-related science that helps to inform and improve all talent management decisions, processes, and programs.

Guardian Career Fields

Essential to the development of Guardians is career field assignment. The CHCO, under SecAF authority, uses the defined developmental categories and specialty codes within each category. The USSF assigns Guardians to one of the core specialties in figure 2 below. Guardian training focuses on developing skills and knowledge required to excel in their assigned specialty area.

Developmental Categories	Core Space Force Specialties
Operations	Astronaut (Officers) Space Operations Intelligence Cyberspace Operations
Force Modernization	Developmental Engineer Acquisition Management

Figure 2. USSF career field designations

Developmental Teams (DT)

DTs manage force development for all Guardians. DTs establish an understanding of both resources and requirements and ensure Guardians in every career field receive appropriate support for their professional development. The USSF uses a comprehensive and individualized approach to personnel development supported by centralized and concurrent boards for promotions, assignments, education, command selection, performance-based retention, development program matches, competency framework adjustments, diversity, and recruiting needs in accordance with all applicable laws and policies. Board members and hiring officials review competencies required to fill projected needs, and consider an individual's personal circumstances and capabilities, and any aspirations they wish to share with the board. While performance is necessary to identify qualified promotion candidates, it does not guarantee the preparedness of individuals to assume increased responsibilities.

Training

Training facilitates development of the necessary knowledge, skills, and abilities for Guardians to execute their role within the USSF, from initial entry to the Service, and throughout their career. Training moves Guardians from initial assessment through advanced skill development. Training also includes specialized skill development for a career field, qualification training for specific duties, tool or weapon system proficiency, or for deployment preparations. Training is not necessarily a sequential process, allowing individuals to request training exemption waivers that allow them to progress to more advanced training or to receive training in a new area. This is particularly true for Guardians transferring from another Service that bring with them extensive knowledge and experience. Guardians will require training throughout their career. Advancement through training courses is not dependent on rank, grade, or time in service.

Competencies and Development

An individual's competencies and experiences drive progress through the training process and achievement of higher tiers of expertise.

- Level 1 – Basic proficiency
- Level 2 – Intermediate proficiency
- Level 3 – Advanced proficiency
- Level 4 – Expert proficiency

Competencies are the knowledge, skills, abilities, and other characteristics necessary to complete tasks. The USSF identifies competencies in two broad categories: foundational and occupational. Foundational competencies or soft skills focus on the human aspects of an individual's strengths, including knowledge, skills, abilities, and other characteristics that transcend occupational knowledge and skills (e.g., character, emotional intelligence).

---

a. **Accession Training.** A new Guardian's first stop is accession training. Accession training establishes a foundational culture common to all Guardians. For enlisted Guardians this is basic military training. Officer accession training is via the individual's commissioning source (military academy, reserve officer training corps, or officer candidate school). Interservice transfers complete a Guardian orientation course.

b. **Individual Skills Training (IST).** Following accession training, Guardians proceed to IST. These specialty-awarding courses provide Guardians the basics of their assigned career fields.

c. **Spacepower Discipline Courses.** The 319th Combat Training Squadron (CTS), part of STARCOM/Delta 1, provides the spacepower discipline (SPD) courses for the USSF. SPD courses are open to all space forces. These courses teach the initial competencies and critical thinking skills for a specific spacepower discipline. There are currently four SPD 100-level courses, covering the disciplines of Orbital Warfare, Space Electronic Warfare, Space Battle Management, and Military Intelligence. The 319 CTS currently offers two SPD-300 courses, on Orbital Warfare and Overhead Persistent Infrared systems. The material in these courses deepens an individual's expertise in a discipline, and helps them understand the link between that discipline and the joint fight.

SPD Courses

The 319 CTS is maturing SPD training and adding new courses. Current SPD-100 level courses will migrate to on-line delivery to simplify participation. SPD-200 and SPD-300 courses will be more in-depth, building on the SPD-100 courses.

---

d. **Mission Qualification Training (MQT).** Following spacepower discipline training, Guardians complete MQT associated with a specific weapon system. MQT often contains a variety of hands-on instruction and simulator or weapon system evaluations that culminate in a certification to operate a weapon system.

e. **Career Specialty and Other Courses.** Guardians will require training beyond the SPD courses throughout their careers, whether to support their specific career field, to prepare for deployment, to maintain proficiency, or to support a new weapon system. The USSF, USAF, other services, and the joint community may provide these courses.

   1) **Astronaut.** Guardians selected for the astronaut program complete required training through the National Aeronautics and Space Administration (NASA) or other agencies as directed.

   2) **Operational TTPs.** The Ready Spacecrew Program focuses on enhancing knowledge and warfighting capability of space forces. Advanced training courses address operational TTPs that include cyberspace and intelligence to prepare space forces to integrate effects across multiple domains and achieve weapon system mastery. Examples of advanced training include, but are not limited to, exercises (e.g., Space Flag), and wargames (e.g., Schriever/STARCOM wargames).

   3) **Intelligence.** Guardians assigned to the intelligence specialty may pursue training through intelligence community sources such as the Defense Intelligence Agency's Joint Military Intelligence Training Center, and the National Security Agency's National Cryptologic School.

4) **Cyberspace Operations.** Guardians assigned to the cyberspace operations specialty can leverage the DOD Cyber Exchange for a wide range of training courses.

5) **Deployment Preparation.** Guardians preparing for deployment receive preparation training, including tactics, techniques, and procedures (TTPs) and combatant commander support, from the 319 CTS. These preparatory courses include the Space Warfighter Preparation Course and Space Flag Preparatory Course. Space forces may also receive training at their deployed location.

6) **Acquisition Management.** Guardians assigned to the acquisition management or developmental engineering specialties can pursue training and certification within one or more of the six functional areas as established by the Under Secretary of Defense for Acquisition and Sustainment. The functional areas are Program Management, Contracting, Life Cycle Logistics, Engineering and Technical Management, Test and Evaluation, Business – Financial Management and Cost Estimating.

7) **Digital Fluency and Supra Coders Courses.** In the USSF's first planning guidance publication, the CSO established his intent to create a digital service to accelerate innovation. This vision applies to all USSF operations, acquisition, engineering, and business processes. The CSO calls on Guardians and other personnel assigned to the USSF, to acquire and use innovative digital skills in their assigned duties regardless of career specialty. Guardian Supra Coders, having completed an intensive software engineering curriculum, become members of agile software development product teams in the field so they can develop, deploy, and update software that works for its users at the speed of mission need. Digital Fluency courses are available through the Digital University (accessible via the Space Force Portal). Supra Coder courses are accessible at https://supracoders.us/.

8) **Other Courses.** Guardians may pursue a variety of other courses as their careers and assignments progress. Among these may be joint courses in planning and targeting.

Education

Building on the knowledge and skills developed through training, formal education hones knowledge, critical and strategic thinking skills, and leadership abilities. An individual attends professional military education (PME), professional continuing education (PCE), or pursues advanced degrees based on demonstrated ability, potential, and readiness to take the next step in leading inclusive, innovative, and agile teams.

a. **PME.** PME programs educate Guardians to leverage military power to achieve national security objectives. Courses such as Airman Leadership School, Noncommissioned

Officer Academy, Senior Noncommissioned Officer Academy, Squadron Officer School, Air Command, and Staff College – Schriever Space Scholars, School of Advanced Air and Space Studies, Air War College – West Space Seminar, and the Joint Professional Military Education courses support Guardians as they progress through the ranks.

b. **PCE.** PCE provides continued professional development for individuals in all specialty areas.

   1) **Space PCE Courses.** National Security Space Institute (NSSI), part of STARCOM Delta 13, provides PCE for all DOD space professionals as well as allies and partners. The NSSI offers a wide range of courses through the College of Professional Development and the College of Space Warfare. Within the College of Professional Development, Space 100 (introduction to space capabilities and operations), Space 200 (space operations and the joint and space planning processes) and Space 300 (capability development, and space policy and strategy) serve to broaden an individual's overall understanding of space, and provide in-depth knowledge of specific topics to satisfy mission accomplishment, sustainment, or enhancement. Other NSSI courses within the College of Professional Development include the Space Executive Course and the Space Capstone Publication Course. Within the College of Space Warfare, existing and emerging courses include Introduction to Space, Space Familiarization Course, Space Intelligence Fundamentals Course, Joint Space Targeting Course, Fundamentals Application Space Targeting Course, Coalition Space Course, Joint Space Planners Course, Joint Integrated Space Team Course, Fundamentals of Orbital Operations Course, Concepts of Orbital Warfare Course, and Global Space Domain Awareness Course. The NSSI continues to develop new courses within both colleges as the need and interest arise.

   2) **Weapons School.** Individuals assigned to space operations, cyberspace operations and intelligence can attend the United States Air Force Weapons School (USAFWS). USAFWS teaches graduate-level courses that provide advanced training in weapons and tactics employment. The 19th Weapons Squadron (WPS) (intelligence), 328 WPS (space), and 32 WPS (cyberspace) support USSF and USAF personnel. Additionally, enlisted space and intelligence personnel can attend the USAFWS Advanced Instructor Course.

   3) **Intelligence.** Guardians assigned to the intelligence specialty may attend a wide variety of courses across the different intelligence disciplines. The 313th Training Squadron at Goodfellow Air Force Base offers the intelligence Basic Career Development Program, Intermediate Career Development Program, and Advanced Career Development Program courses. Additionally, enlisted intelligence personnel can apply to attend the National Intelligence University for Bachelor's or Master's degrees in a select field of study.

4) **Cyberspace Operations.** Guardians assigned to the cyberspace operations specialty may pursue PCE courses through the Air Force Institute of Technology (AFIT) School of Systems and Logistics or the School of Strategic Force Studies.

> **Intelligence and Cyberspace Education**
> STARCOM recognizes the need to extend intelligence and cyberspace advanced training to meet the growing requirements of the USSF. Future intelligence and cyberspace courses for Guardians may fall under the USAFWS to promote continued integration within the DAF.

5) **Acquisition Management and Developmental Engineering.** Guardians assigned to the acquisition management and developmental engineering specialties may pursue courses through Defense Acquisition University, the AFIT School of Systems and Logistics, or acquisition courses offered by other services or other government agencies.

6) **Acquisition Instructor Course (AQIC).** AQIC develops acquisition officers as expert instructors and integrators. Instruction focuses on instructorship, operational integration, and critical thinking

7) **USAF Test Pilot School Space Test Course.** The Space Test Course offers a rigorous education in test fundamentals, systems testing, and space sciences.

c. **Advanced Degrees.** Guardians can attend AFIT or the Naval Postgraduate School for space, cyberspace, engineering, and acquisition related degree programs. Individuals may also pursue other degree programs through traditional colleges and universities that support their professional and personal development goals. Guardians also have access to a variety of science, technology, engineering and math degree programs, and space research opportunities, through the USSF's University Partnership Program. While the nature of space operations means that science, technology, engineering and math degrees are most applicable to daily requirements, space forces are encouraged to pursue degrees in other fields of interest as well.

Experience

Experience contributes to an individual's development in ways that neither training nor education can. Diverse experiences enable Guardians to be more effective team members. This experience may come from operational experience on the job, experience developed while part of another Service, internships, education with industry (EWI), or other experience in the commercial sector. Guardians are encouraged to take advantage of the unique opportunities for development that come with assignments including those listed below:

- Joint assignments

- USAF assignments (such as at Air Force Research Laboratory (AFRL))

- Training assignments

- Recruiting assignments

- Deployments

- Participation in partnerships with our allies and international partners

- Engagements with allies and partners through wargames and exercises

- Liaison positions with other agencies

- EWI

- Engagements with academia (Seminars, Reserve Officers' Training Corps (ROTC) instructor, or instructor at the United States Air Force Academy)

Chapter 4: Guardian Resilience

The USSF's mission and commitment to serve our nation can be challenging and stressful to Guardians and their families. Developing individual resilience involves building skills to establish behaviors, and patterns of thought and action, which promote personal wellbeing and mental health. Resilience — an individual's capacity to recover from hardship or difficulties — is a critical element of readiness. People can develop the ability to withstand, adapt to, and recover from stress and adversity by using effective coping strategies. Thus, strengthening resilience has a direct impact on the lethality and effectiveness of a warfighting unit. Those who are physically, mentally, spiritually, emotionally, or financially overwhelmed may struggle to adapt and fail to perform successfully in dynamic and stressful environments. Safeguarding and strengthening resilience extends beyond the readiness imperative and constitutes a solemn commitment embraced by every leader.

The USSF is committed to providing this support to all Guardians and those forces attached or assigned to the USSF. A variety of programs including those detailed below, and equal opportunity, counseling, mental health support, and financial support, provide Guardians the means to develop resilience (physically, mentally, spiritually, or emotionally) or to deal with challenging situations.

Coaching and Mentoring

Coaching and mentoring programs, accessible through TMO, are central to continuous development and engagement. Mentorship programs match a Guardian to another more experienced Guardian who can share perspectives and insight. Coaching programs focus on helping Guardians improve in desired areas of their personal lives and professional performance. Mentorship and coaching programs supplement leadership efforts to address Guardian needs for individualized and small group support.

Diversity and Inclusion

A diverse, inclusive force is one strengthened by a myriad of unique perspectives and experiences. The Assistant Secretary of the Air Force for Diversity and Inclusion (SAF/DI) provides guidance, direction, and support to both USAF and USSF personnel. Diversity education and training is critical to the development of our Guardians at every stage of their careers to meet emerging operational challenges. Cultivating diversity acumen fosters an inclusive culture in which members of different groups bring diverse knowledge and perspectives to the organization. The SAF/DI office will assist STARCOM as needed with curriculum, content, and methodology for training Guardians. These efforts will set a strong foundation for Guardians to lead diverse teams in an increasingly competitive and dynamic global environment.

Sexual Assault and Harassment Prevention

"Each member of our team shares in the enduring responsibility to eliminate sexual assault and harassment from our ranks. I urge every Airman, Guardian, and Department civilian to treat each other with dignity and respect, hold others accountable to our high standards of conduct, and to take care of your teammates." SecAF Frank Kendall, 27 April 2022

Sexual harassment and assault undermine the cohesion, readiness, and morale of the force. Every Guardian has a role to play in fighting the crime of sexual assault. SecAF Frank Kendall signed a proclamation, on 27 April 2022, reaffirming DAF's commitment to preventing sexual assault and sexual harassment, and to supporting sexual assault survivors. Sexual Assault Prevention and Response (SAPR) supports Guardians in working to eliminate sexual assault in the Space Force. SAPR and Family Advocacy Programs support Guardians and other forces assigned to the USSF, and their families who are victims of sexual assault. SAPR provides support for adult sexual assault victims when the perpetrator is someone other than the victim's spouse or domestic partner. The Family Advocacy Program manages sexual assault allegations when the alleged offender is the partner in the context of a spousal relationship, domestic partnership, unmarried intimate partner relationship, or when the victim is a military dependent 17 years of age or younger.

Suicide and Violence Prevention

Losing a Guardian or family member to death by suicide or a violent event can have a significant impact on an organization's morale and readiness. The USSF's Prevention Team supports Guardians and other forces assigned to the USSF, and their families by creating a primary prevention program for interpersonal and self-directed violence, including domestic violence, child abuse, sexual assault, sexual harassment, and suicide.

Other Programs

a. **Family and Spouse Support Programs.** There are a variety of other programs including the Exceptional Family Member Program, Key Spouse Program, Spouse Education and Career Opportunities program, Priority Placement Program, Join-Spouse Program, Childcare Development Center, and Guardian Family Career Program, which support Guardians and their families.

b. **Morale, Welfare, and Recreation (MWR) Office.** MWR on Air Force and Space Force bases offers a variety of programs for Guardians and their families that support readiness and resilience. These include intramural sports, life skills programs, personal health and wellness programs, fitness programs, the hobby shop, religious services and programs, childcare, and other programs and events for children and teens.

c. **Air Force Services Center (AFSVC).** AFSVC offers a variety of programs at Air Force and Space Force bases intended to build a resilient force through creative customer-driven recreational programs for Guardians and their families both on and off the installation. These programs include aero clubs, bowling, exercise facilities, combined clubs, golf courses, event tickets, and travel.

d. **ESport/Space Force Gaming.** Also managed by AFSVC, Air Force Gaming and Space Force Gaming are the official ESport gaming programs and competition hub for the USAF and USSF. ESport is a program designed to bolster resilience, forge camaraderie, and hone warrior-lethality in preparation for the future fight. Twice a year, Airmen and Guardians from around the world compete in the DAF Gaming League in order to find the best in the DAF.

Chapter 5: Global Perspective

Guardians must develop and maintain a global perspective in order to provide innovative solutions and spacepower effects for the US and our allies. Guardians must be sufficiently agile to leverage joint, interagency, allied, civil, and/or commercial resources. Our global persistence and enduring vigilance posture the joint force to assure allies, deter aggression, coerce competitors, and defeat adversaries. USSF training, education, and readiness inculcate Guardians with an understanding of joint planning, doctrine, and partnerships/engagements (multinational, interagency, academia, and industry) in order to advance national priorities as part of the joint force.

Engaging with the Joint Community

The USSF organizes, trains, and equips Guardians to provide capabilities to meet joint force requirements in support of the National Defense Strategy. Through their training, education, and experience, Guardians master concepts, doctrine, and practices as joint warfighters to maximize the power of integration with the Army, Navy, Air Force, Marine Corps, and Coast Guard. Guardians also focus on addressing threats and risks affecting our capabilities and forces, and institute mitigation steps in order to ensure our competitive advantage.

Guardians exercise close integration with their service and combatant command partners at all echelons of joint command. This includes participation in the planning, conduct, and assessment of operations to deliver space effects to all domains, to protect and defend space capabilities, and deny the advantage to the adversary. Joint integration is crucial to employing space expertise in the joint forces' synchronization, planning, and execution efforts. The USSF training and education includes the USSF planning process, as described in SDP 5-0, *Planning*, to prepare Guardians to engage with other services and the joint community.

Multinational Partnerships - Our Allies and Partners

Every day, Guardians take action and make decisions that can have international consequences. Expanding our cooperation with allies and partners to enhance prosperity and security is a priority for the USSF identified by the CSO. Deliberate engagements with our treaty allies and partners orient our responsibilities to enhance deterrence, protect mutual interests, assure access, and build capability and capacity for a common purpose. Guardians engage with our allies and partners to establish common norms of behavior, and to understand the unique backgrounds and the capabilities they bring to space in the combined fight. These partnerships may extend to foreign military, civil, and commercial entities as necessary to provide the USSF operational and strategic advantages in the space domain.

Guardians at every skill level and from every space discipline can have the opportunity to engage with allies and partners in several ways. Examples of such duties include:

a. **Mobile Training Teams.** These are short-term duties where Guardians engage foreign partners for a specific purpose, such as new equipment training, cultural alignment, or doctrinal exchange.

b. **Military Personnel Exchange Program.** These are positions, managed at the SecAF level, that directly exchange Guardians with a foreign command. Guardians fulfill their duties as a part of that organization. The foreign command reciprocates by assigning personnel to a position within a USSF organization. Both units benefit from the experience of being part of an international team.

c. **Liaison Officers (LNO).** The USSF selects Guardians to represent either the Service or a subordinate Field Command to an allied or partner organization. They are the "on the ground" resource for allies and partners to engage the USSF. LNOs reduce friction and synchronize action between their sending and receiving commands.

d. **Security Cooperation Officers.** Assigned as a staff member to a US Embassy Country Team, these Guardians coordinate and execute the Service's security cooperation programs directly with the government and militaries of allied and partner nations.

e. **Study Abroad.** These programs offer Guardians extended immersion in a foreign culture at an institution of higher learning. Study abroad programs allow participants to make personal connections with academic, civil, and commercial space experts outside of the United States. Guardians return to the USSF with increased knowledge and insights earned through the experience.

f. **Regional Space Advisor (RSA) Program.** The RSA Program identifies and prepares a select group of Guardians for direct interaction with allies and partners. RSAs form a cadre of Guardian leaders deliberately developed to enhance USSF capabilities by evolving and expanding partnerships to strengthen relationships, secure common interests, and promote shared values in space. As a career-broadening program, USSF expects RSAs to demonstrate proficiency in a core space discipline and receive additional training to increase their personal leadership competencies. With advanced knowledge of space policies and political-military affairs, regional and cultural expertise, and demonstrated language proficiency (as needed), the USSF assigns RSA to key strategic billets. In those roles, RSAs implement campaign support plans and inject, track, and assess the USSF's space domain interests within both regional theater security cooperation plans, and allied and partner nation activities.

Interagency, Industry, and Academic Engagements

USSF interagency, academic, and industry engagements are key components to strengthening our overall capabilities. Guardians with exposure to other government agencies as LNOs, in joint or interagency assignments, working in a DAF organization such as AFRL or at the LeMay Center, or through other engagements gain valuable experience while providing space expertise to these organizations. For example, today there are Guardians assigned to the National

Reconnaissance Office, National Geospatial-Intelligence Agency, National Air and Space Intelligence Center, the Department of Commerce, and NASA. Guardians can also participate in EWI to develop first-hand knowledge of industry capabilities and processes. The USSF has established developmental partnerships with a network of universities that can provide world-class space research and professional development opportunities. These outreach relationships enable the USSF to foster a diverse, highly technical, and specialized workforce. The aim is to collaborate, as permitted by law and policy, on the long and short-term science and technology (S&T) problem sets; and to promote partnerships with academic institutions, government labs, and private industry. This collaborative and inclusive approach allows the USSF to promote and strengthen strategic relationships to deliver new capabilities at operationally relevant speeds that enhance security and preserve prosperity of the space domain.

a. **University Partnership Program (UPP).** The UPP aims to establish strategic partnerships with some of the nation's top universities that possess high academic standards, nationally-ranked Science, Technology, Engineering, and Mathematics (STEM) degree programs, world-renowned space-related research, and established ROTC detachments. The UPP's objectives are to develop a highly competent and diverse workforce; advance strategic focus areas and pursue critical S&T topics that are significant to the USSF; and create workforce development and advanced academic degree opportunities for Guardians. In addition, the UPP provides scholarships, internships and mentorship programs for university students and ROTC cadets with the goal of recruiting and developing diverse Guardians with a particular focus on STEM and space disciplines.

b. **University Consortium (UC).** A vital component of the UPP, the UC represents an opportunity for universities to contribute to USSF's S&T priorities. The purpose of the UC is to connect universities to DOD space research and transition opportunities to USSF, communicate problem focus areas to space consortium members, and foster collaboration between universities, government, and industry. Additionally, the collaboration with government laboratories, including Air Force Research Laboratory, Naval Research Laboratory, Army Research Laboratory, Department of Energy, National Aeronautics and Space Administration, industry and international research institutions, aims to provide research and infrastructure to accelerate innovation and transition and foster space workforce development.

Chapter 6: USAF Support to the USSF

The USSF, as part of the DAF, employs Guardians, active-duty Airmen, DAF civilians, Air Force Reservists and Air National Guardsmen to execute the space mission. DAF Airmen and civilians also provide installation and facilities support for Garrisons and Space Force Bases.

Personnel Serving in USSF Organizations

a. **Active-duty Airmen.** Active-duty Airmen serve in all the space specialties. Active-duty Airmen also provide essential services at the Space Force Base and Garrison levels. AFPC and SAF/A1 handle personnel matters for Airmen assigned to the USSF or stationed on Space Force Bases.

b. **Civilians.** Civilian Guardians are members of the DAF. Civilians assigned to the USSF work at all levels of the service, including all space specialties. DAF civilians also provide essential services at the Space Force Base and Garrison levels. The USSF civilian personnel office (SF/S1C) is an extension of the DAF and is responsible for managing civilians assigned to the USSF in space specialty career fields. AFPC, AF/A1, and TMO handle personnel matters for all other DAF civilians supporting Garrisons or stationed on Space Force Bases. DAF civilian Career Field Teams manage civilian professional development through input from USSF career field leadership and talent managers. Civilian Guardians participate in DAF civilian development programs, development teams, and selection processes composed of boards and panels that include USSF senior leaders.

c. **Air Force Reserve (AFR).** The AFR is part of the reserve component of the USAF. Air Force Reservists, including Individual Mobilization Augmentees, enable surge capacity, conduct operations, and provide operational support for USSF missions. These forces remain in the Air Force and follow Air Force personnel processes and policies. The AFR provides follow-on forces to meet any joint force mission. The AFR allows the USSF to leverage industry experience as a force multiplier, enables a continuum of service, and provides expanded talent management options for the force.

d. **Air National Guard (ANG).** ANG is part of the reserve component of the USAF. Control of ANG units may alternate between their state governments and the federal government. The ANG is currently performing space missions in command and control, intelligence, space electromagnetic warfare, staff augmentation, and missile warning. The ANG builds partnerships at the international, federal, state, and local levels to contribute to the nation's strength and readiness.

> ### Development of Air Reserve Component Space Professionals
> Today AFR and ANG space professionals remain part of the USAF. The USSF is developing processes and policies to ensure a common presentation of forces to combatant commanders, and preservation of capability among forces performing space missions. Coordination with the AFR and ANG to identify impacts to mission capability remains critical as the USSF grows.

USAF Organizations Supporting the USSF

USAF organizations provide many of the personnel functions for Guardians and USAF, AFR, and ANG personnel assigned to USSF units or Space Force Bases. In addition to the personnel support functions detailed below, USAF also provides legal, religious affairs, finance, contracting, meteorological, and mortuary affairs support to Guardians.

a. **Air Force Offices.** AF/A1, SAF/MR, and SAF/AQ in coordination with SF/S1, provide oversight for all DAF manpower, personnel, and service activities. These roles include policy development and oversight of DAF manpower (military and civilian personnel), reserve component affairs, the Acquisition Demonstration program, equal opportunity and diversity, medical readiness and health programs, family advocacy and readiness programs, sexual assault prevention and response, base services, exchanges, commissaries, and MWR programs.

b. **AFPC.** AFPC provides operational oversight, instructions, and guidance to USSF and its FIELDCOMs for Guardians and Airmen assigned to USSF units. AFPC in conjunction with offices under the SF/S1 manages assignments for Guardians assigned to the USSF.

c. **Air Force Materiel Command (AFMC).** AFMC is the servicing major command for installation and facilities operations on Space Force Bases. AFMC is responsible for ensuring Airmen assigned to USSF Garrisons receive the same force development opportunities, and functional and administrative support, as those at USAF installations.

d. **Air Force Reserve Command (AFRC).** AFRC provides operational oversight, instructions, and guidance to USSF and its FIELDCOMs including operating procedures to implement and maintain guidance. Air Reserve Personnel Center (ARPC) provides record keeping for Air Force Reserve (AFR) and Air National Guard personnel. AFR members assigned to USSF organizations formulate and implement policy, guidance, and resources pertaining to AFR forces, and advise USSF leadership on the operational employment of Reservists.

e. **National Guard Bureau (NGB).** The NGB provides resources, policy oversight, and guidance to ensure Air National Guard personnel are ready, trained, and equipped for homeland and global operations. Guardsmen assigned to USSF organizations provide advice and assistance on NGB matters affecting the USSF. They synchronize NGB and USSF efforts, support unit readiness, and plan optimal integration into future missions.

Appendix A: Acronyms and Abbreviations

AFIT	Air Force Institute of Technology
AFPC	Air Force Personnel Center
AFMC	Air Force Materiel Command
AFR	Air Force Reserve
AFRC	Air Force Reserve Command
AFSVC	Air Force Services Center
ANG	Air National Guard
AFRL	Air Force Research Laboratory
AQIC	Acquisition Instructor Course
ARPC	Air Reserve Personnel Center
C-FLDCOM	component - field command
CHCO	Chief Human Capital Officer (SF/S1)
CMSSF	Chief Master Sergeant of the Space Force
CSO	Chief of Space Operations
CTS	Combat Training Squadron
DAF	Department of the Air Force
DOD	Department of Defense
EWI	Education with Industry
FIELDCOM	field command
IST	Individual Skills Training
LNO	Liaison Officers
MQT	Mission Qualification Training
NASA	National Aeronautics and Space Administration
NGB	National Guard Bureau
NSSI	National Security Space Institute
PCE	professional continuing education
PME	professional military education

MWR	Morale, Welfare, and Recreation
ROTC	Reserve Officers' Training Corps
RSA	Regional Space Advisor
S&T	science and technology
SAF	Secretary of the Air Force
SAF/AQ	Assistant Secretary of the Air Force for Acquisition, Technology, and Logistics
SAF/DI	Assistant Secretary of the Air Force for Diversity and Inclusion
SAF/MR	Assistant Secretary of the Air Force Manpower & Reserve
SAPR	Sexual Assault Prevention and Response
SDP	Space Doctrine Publication
SecAF	Secretary of the Air Force
SFELM	Space Force Element
SPD	spacepower discipline
SpOC	Space Operations Command
SSC	Space Systems Command
STARCOM	Space Training and Readiness Command
STEM	Science, Technology, Engineering and Mathematics
TMO	Talent Management Office
TTP	tactics, techniques and procedures
UC	University Consortium
UPP	University Partnership Program
USAF	United States Air Force
USAFWS	United States Air Force Weapons School
USSF	United States Space Force
VCSO	Vice Chief of Space Operations
WPS	Weapons Squadron